For the wave riders
and those who hold out their hands.
— JH

For activists everywhere.
— CC

Text copyright © 2023 by Joanna Ho
Illustrations copyright © 2023 by Cátia Chien
All photos courtesy of Ai Weiwei Studio

ISBN 978-1-338-71594-1
10 9 8 7 6 5 4 3 2 1   23 24 25 26 27
Printed in Malaysia   162 • First edition, October 2023
Book design by Doan Buu
The text type was set in Futura. The display type was set in Billy The Flying Robot and altered in Photoshop.
The illustrations were created using pencils, pastels, and Photoshop.

Resources: Documentaries — Johnsen, Andreas, director. *Ai Weiwei: The Fake Case*. BBC, 2013. 86 minutes. | Klayman, Alison, director. *Ai Weiwei: Never Sorry*. IFC Films, 2012. 91 minutes. | Springford, Matthew, director. *Ai Weiwei: Without Fear or Favor*. BBC, 2010. 60 minutes. | Weiwei, Ai, director. *Ai Weiwei: So Sorry*. Ai Weiwei Studio, 2012. 55 minutes. | Weiwei, Ai, director. *Human Flow*. AC Films, 2017. 140 minutes.| Books — Martin, Barnaby. *Hanging Man: The Arrest of Ai Weiwei*. Farrar, Straus and Giroux, 2013. | Articles — Block, Melissa. "In 'According to What?' Ai Weiwei Makes Mourning Subversive." NPR, January 23, 2013. http://www.npr.org/2013/01/23/169973843/in-according-to-what-ai-wei-wei-makes-mourning-subversive | "China Artist Ai Weiwei Says He Regrets Designing Beijing Olympics Bird's Nest." *Telegraph*, March 5, 2012. https://www.telegraph.co.uk/culture/art/art-news/9123705/China-artist-Ai-Weiwei-says-he-regrets-designing-Beijing-Olympics-Birds-Nest.html | "Documenting the Story of Ai Weiwei." PBS Thirteen. https://www.pbs.org/wgbh/pages/frontline/ai-wei-wei/ai-weiwei-story | Etherington, Rose. "Sunflower Seeds 2010 by Ai Weiwei." *Dezeen*, October 11, 2020. https://www.dezeen.com/2010/10/11/sunflower-seeds-2010-by-ai-weiwei/# | Kinsella, Eileen. "Free to Travel Once More, Ai Weiwei Is Having a Huge New York Moment." *Artnet*, November 5, 2015. https://news.artnet.com/art-world/ai-weiwei-four-nyc-shows-733172 | Lesser, Casey. "Ai Weiwei Returns to New York with Powerful Shows at Deitch Projects, Mary Boone, and Lisson." Artsy.net, November 7, 2016. https://www.artsy.net/article/artsy-editorial-ai-weiwei-returns-to-new-york-with-four-powerful-shows | Osnos, Evan. "It's Not Beautiful." *New Yorker*, May 17, 2010. https://www.newyorker.com/magazine/2010/05/24/its-not-beautiful | Phillips, Tom. "Ai Weiwei Free to Travel Overseas Again after China Returns His Passport." *Guardian*, July 22, 2015. https://www.theguardian.com/artanddesign/2015/jul/22/ai-weiwei-free-to-travel-overseas-again-after-china-returns-his-passport | Pogrebin, Robin. "Ai Weiwei Melds Art and Activism in Shows about Displacement." *New York Times*, October 20, 2016. https://www.nytimes.com/2016/10/21/arts/design/ai-weiwei-melds-art-and-activism-in-shows-about-displacement.html | "Sichuan 2008: A Disaster on an Immense Scale." BBC, May 9, 2013. https://www.bbc.com/news/science-environment-22398684 | Stinson, Liv. "Ai Weiwei's Shockingly Detailed Remake of His Life in a Chinese Prison." *Wired*, June 26, 2013. https://www.wired.com/2013/06/ai-weiweis-self-referential-work-in-venice/ | Weiwei, Ai. "The Refugee Crisis Isn't about Refugees. It's about Us." *Guardian*, February 2, 2018. https://www.theguardian.com/commentisfree/2018/feb/02/refugee-crisis-human-flow-ai-weiwei-china | Weiwei, Ai. "Why I'll Stay Away from the Opening Ceremony of the Olympics." *Guardian*, August 7, 2008. https://www.theguardian.com/commentisfree/2008/aug/07/olympics2008.china | Wong, Edward. "Chinese Authorities Raze an Artist's Studio." *New York Times*, January 12, 2011. https://www.nytimes.com/2011/01/13/world/asia/13china.html | Wong, Edward. "First a Black Hood, Then 81 Captive Days for an Artist in China." *New York Times*, May 26, 2012. https://www.nytimes.com/2012/05/27/world/asia/first-a-black-hood-then-81-captive-days-for-artist-in-china.html | Yau, John. "Ai Weiwei New York Photographs 1983–1993." *Brooklyn Rail*, September 2011. https://brooklynrail.org/2011/09/artseen/ai-weiwei-new-york-photographs-1983-1993 | Zand, Bernhard. "Ai Weiwei's New Life in Europe." *Der Spiegel International*, August 13, 2015. https://www.spiegel.de/international/world/artist-ai-weiwei-has-left-china-for-germany-a-1047793.html

ON THE TIP OF A WAVE

How Ai Weiwei's Art Is Changing the Tide

written by Joanna Ho

illustrated by Cátia Chien

Orchard Books

Scholastic Inc. | New York

Ai Weiwei
waited on the rocky shore,
waded into the wet,
and watched as a boat
teetered and tottered
on precarious waves
that propelled it toward the shore.

Cradling the
memories,

fears,

hopes,

and dreams

of its passengers,
the rubber raft sank low
low
low
into the sea,
barely holding itself
above water.

Ai Weiwei
held out his hands
as those who rode the waves
leapt onto the land.

Splashing,
      sploshing,
            he helped as
                  mothers
                        passed
                              babies
                                    to
                                          fathers
                                                who passed
                                                      their
                                                            precious cargo
                                                                  to
                                                                        strangers
                                                                              standing on a strange land
                                                                                    with extended
                                                                                          hands.

Ai Weiwei knew
surviving the sea
was only the beginning.

So, he offered tea
as the wave riders
trekked on without directions,
only hope
that each step
would bring them closer to a better life.
Left behind on the beach,
their life jackets piled high —
a neon mountain
reaching to the heavens
like a prayer.

He felt the life jackets
and an idea curled and crested
through his fingertips.
The way it always did.

Like the mothers
        and fathers
              and children
                    he held on the shore,
Ai Weiwei knew what it was
to live on the tip of a wave,
far from home
and always in danger.

Ai Weiwei had learned
to use his hands
in a hole in the ground
on the edge of a dusty desert.

Beneath the labor camp
where childhood blew past
    him like sand,
he found refuge
by turning his dirt walls
into art.

When his stomach growled,
he sculpted.
When his spirit was crushed,
he shaped.
Under the weight of injustice,
he created.

He discovered dignity
in his hands.
Using ordinary objects,
Ai Weiwei challenged others
to see the world differently.

A coat hanger.

Hanging Man
1985

A shoe.

One Man Shoe
1987

A vase.

Dropping a Han Dynasty Urn
1995

Nine thousand backpacks.

Remembering
2009

One hundred million hand-painted porcelain sunflower seeds.

Too many toy bricks to count.

Trace
2014

KONZERT

And now,
several thousand life jackets
    salvaged from a neon mountain
    on an island
    in the Aegean Sea.

Six columns
    standing at attention
    on the steps
    of a German concert house.

AUS BERLIN

One
by
one
each life jacket
was lifted and tied
to its neighbor —
foam vests
wrapped around
stone pillars,
holding on to
one another
to stay
afloat.

One crane
and a tireless team
working overnight
on the eve of a movie gala
hosting enough stars
to fill the sky.

The next day,
onlookers and
gala-goers gawked.

They gaped.

They gasped.

They remembered
the wave riders
the world seemed to forget.

Safe Passage
2016

Intertwined, the life jackets
pleaded for safe passage
on behalf of those
carried far from home
by currents
they could not control.

Neon prayers
lifted to the heavens,
imploring hearts
and hands
and doors
and borders
to open

one
by
one
by
one
by
one.

Ai Weiwei
lived on the tip of a wave.
It crashed
and ebbed
and once,

it swallowed him whole.

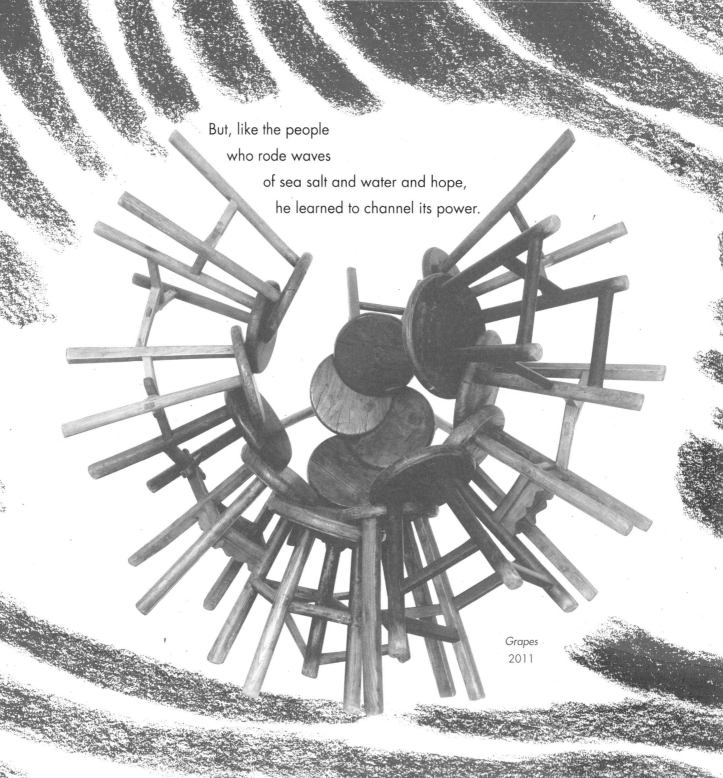

But, like the people
who rode waves
of sea salt and water and hope,
he learned to channel its power.

Grapes
2011

See No Evil, Hear No Evil, Speak No Evil
2009

He reshaped objects and **challenged the world to see differently**.

Han Jar Overpainted with Coca-Cola Logo
1995

Violin
1985

Human Flow
2017

He created art and **invited the world to take action**.

The Rest
2019

The wave rider held out his hands
and helped the world
remember
humanity.

AI WEIWEI

Artist and Activist

Ai Weiwei was born in 1957; when he was one year old, Chinese authorities sent his family to a labor camp to purge intellectuals — writers, artists, teachers, journalists — who were critical of the government. At the time, Ai Weiwei's father was one of the most renowned poets in China, and he became the target of public humiliation and violence. One year later, authorities moved the family to a village near the Gurbantünggüt Desert, where they lived in an underground hole. As a child, Ai Weiwei sculpted dirt walls to remember his own dignity.

For nearly twenty years, Ai Weiwei and his family suffered constant injustice at the labor camp. His mother said that their family "lived on the tip of a wave, always in danger."

In 1981, Ai Weiwei moved to the United States to study art. He returned to Beijing in 1993, to be with his sick father. Life in China shocked him after life in New York. He began to criticize the government.

Freedom is a pretty strange thing. Once you've experienced it, it remains in your heart and no one can take it away. Then as an individual you can be more powerful than a whole country.
— Ai Weiwei

On April 3, 2011, officers secretly detained Ai Weiwei and held him in a secret location without formal charges. Protests erupted around the world, and political leaders called for his release. In the dark of night, eighty-one days after he disappeared, guards dropped Ai Weiwei outside his house.

Authorities took Ai Weiwei's passport and stationed officers around his home, but even under constant surveillance, he kept creating. Though unable to leave Beijing, he continued to speak through artistic exhibitions around the world.

Bird's Nest, 2008

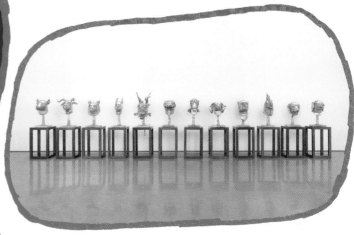

Circle of Animals/Zodiac Heads: Gold, 2010

Trace, 2014

Law of the Journey, 2017

Good Fences Make Good Neighbors, 2017

Safe Passage, 2016

In July 2015, Chinese authorities returned Ai Weiwei's passport, and he moved to Germany. His exile from China overlapped with the refugee crisis in Europe. He began to focus his art on global humanitarian issues and the personal connection to the refugees' pain and struggle. As a child, Ai Weiwei experienced the powerlessness of being displaced from home. As an adult, he experienced the dehumanization of being displaced from country.

Ai Weiwei used life jackets discarded by people passing through the Greek island of Lesbos to create his 2016 installation *Safe Passage*. In 2017, he produced and directed *Human Flow*, a documentary that showed the personal impact and global scale of the refugee crisis across twenty-three countries and more than forty refugee camps. In 2019, he released *The Rest*, a second documentary that depicted the personal stories and impact of refugee conditions around the world.

Human Flow, 2017

A Global Humanitarian Crisis

In the years since Ai Weiwei's first *Safe Passage* installation, conditions for refugees trying to pass through Lesbos have deteriorated. People who survived the treacherous journey to the Greek island have been met with protests, tear gas, and closed European borders. Unsupported and repelled from all directions, over 19,000 wave riders remain trapped in the Moria refugee camp on Lesbos, which was built to hold only 3,000 people. As persecution and violence continue in countries including Syria, Sudan, Somalia, and Afghanistan, more people pour into Moria every day.

The situation in Greece is not unique. The genocide led by the Myanmar government against the Muslim Rohingya displaced over one million people across Asia. In the United States, anti-immigrant rhetoric and inhumane policies like separating families at the southern border and incarcerating immigrant children punish people for seeking asylum. In 2020, at a time when worldwide refugee numbers reached their highest levels since World War II, the United States admitted the lowest number of refugees in forty years. It's hard to believe that not long ago, the United States used to admit more refugees than all other countries combined.

The Rest, 2019

Holding Out Our Hands

Establishing the understanding that we all belong to one humanity is the most essential step for how we might continue to coexist on this sphere we call Earth. There are many borders to dismantle, but the most important are the ones within our own hearts and minds — these are the borders that are dividing humanity from itself.
— Ai Weiwei

Since 2019, Ai Weiwei has lived and worked in different places, including Germany, the United Kingdom, and Portugal. He continues to create art centered on human rights, injustice, and freedom. In 2020, the Minneapolis Institute of Art displayed his *Safe Passage* installation to highlight the ongoing refugee crisis around the world. Minnesota has the highest number of refugees per capita of any state in the United States. Ai Weiwei's art and activism call on us, the citizens of the world, to lift each other up. We must hold out our hands and help each other remember humanity.

The Rest, 2019